SATURN

SATURN

SEYMOUR SIMON

WILLIAM MORROW AND COMPANY, INC.
New York

PHOTO CREDITS

All photographs courtesy of NASA, except page 6,
courtesy of Kyle Cudworth, The Yerkes Observatory.
Art on page 16 by Frank Schwarz.

Printed by New Interlitho, Milan

2 3 4 5 6 7 8 9 10

Library of Congress Cataloging in Publication Data
Simon, Seymour.   Saturn.
Summary: Describes the sixth planet from the sun,
its rings, and its moons, and includes
photographs taken in outer space.
1. Saturn (Planet) — Juvenile literature.
[1. Saturn (Planet)]   I. Title.
QB671.S56 1985   523.4'6   85-2995
ISBN 0-688-05798-5
ISBN 0-688-05799-3 (lib. bdg.)

To Michael Alan Simon

Saturn looks like a faint star in the night sky. But early sky-watchers saw that Saturn and four other stars seemed to move slowly in the night sky. These "stars" were called planets, from a Greek word that means wanderers.

Saturn is a planet. It was named after the Roman god of farming.

oday we know that there are at least nine planets in our Solar System. These planets travel around the sun in paths called orbits. Earth is the third closest planet to the sun. Saturn is the sixth planet from the sun.

Saturn is about 890 million miles from the sun. Saturn is so far away in space that it takes nearly thirty years for it to orbit the sun once.

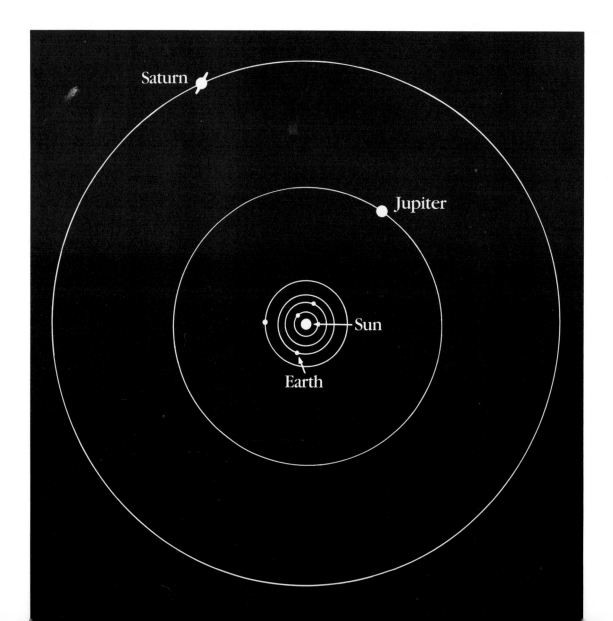

Three unmanned spaceships — *Pioneer 11* and *Voyagers 1 and 2* — have been launched to study Saturn. In 1980, *Voyager 1* took this photograph of the planet and one of its moons. *Voyager 1* traveled much faster than even the fastest jet plane, yet it still took more than three years to reach the distant planet.

Saturn is a giant planet, the second largest after Jupiter. If Saturn were hollow, about 750 planet Earths could fit inside. Like Jupiter, Saturn is made up mostly of gases. This makes it very light for its size. If you could find an ocean large enough, Saturn would float on the water.

Saturn spins around very quickly, once in a little over ten hours. Earth turns around once in twenty-four hours. So Saturn's day is less than one-half of our day.

If you were on the surface of Saturn, you would weigh only a bit more than you would on Earth's surface. For example, if you weigh 100 pounds on Earth, you would weigh about 115 pounds on Saturn.

The great scientist Galileo first saw Saturn through his low-power telescope in the year 1610. He was shocked to see what looked like ears on either side of the planet. Galileo then decided that Saturn was really one large globe and the "ears" were two smaller ones on either side. About fifty years later, an astronomer with a stronger telescope saw that the two smaller globes were really a flat ring around the planet.

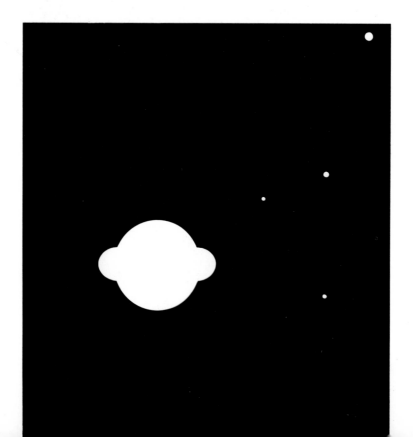

At that time, people were puzzled: Why was Saturn the only planet to have a ring? Nowadays we know that it isn't. In the 1970s, Uranus and Jupiter were discovered to have rings. And scientists suspect that Neptune also has rings.

But the rings of Saturn are still a puzzle. They are the largest rings of any planet. Where did they come from?

If you look through a powerful telescope on Earth, Saturn looks like it has three or four rings. Perhaps you might be able to see five or six. The rings are difficult to see from Earth, and it's not clear how many there are.

The *Pioneer* and *Voyager* spacecraft gave us our first close-up look at the rings. Their photos show that the large rings are made of thousands of smaller rings. There are so many rings that they look like the grooves in a phonograph record.

The rings are made of pieces of ice. Some are as small as your fingernail, others are as big as a house. The rings also contain dust and bits of rock. And all of the material in the rings orbits Saturn like millions of tiny moons.

The pieces in the rings are kept from spinning off into space by the strong pull of Saturn's gravity. Gravity is an invisible force that makes raindrops and snow crystals fall to the ground. Gravity also brings you down when you jump. Gravity pulls everything down toward the center of planet Earth. In the same way, Saturn's gravity pulls everything toward the center of that planet.

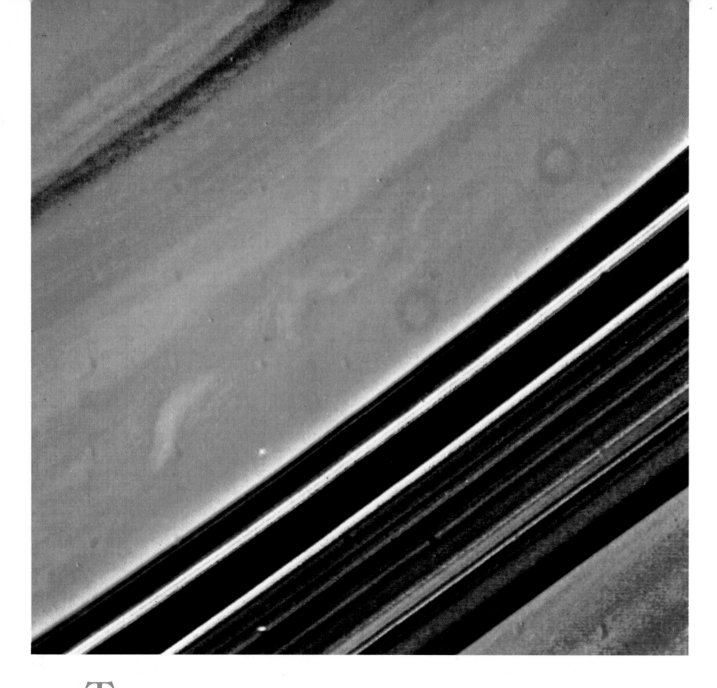

This photo shows part of Saturn's clouds and the beginning of the rings. The ring system starts with a few particles not far above the cloud tops and goes out at least 150 thousand miles into space.

The rings are wide but not very thick. If you see them from the side, they almost disappear. Most of the rings are under three miles thick. And some are much thinner, under two hundred yards thick.

Why are the rings so thin? How did they form? Why are they grouped the way they are? These are just some of the questions that scientists are still puzzling over.

Saturn is made up mostly of gases and liquids. Like Jupiter, Saturn is covered by bands of clouds that circle the planet. But Saturn's clouds are much paler than Jupiter's and are covered by haze. This photo was taken with special filters that make the clouds easy to see.

Saturn is very cold because it is so far away from the sun and receives very little heat. Temperatures on Saturn are more than 300 degrees (F) below zero. That's much colder than the coldest place on Earth. Scientists think Saturn's clouds are mostly frozen crystals of poisonous gases such as ammonia and methane.

A close-up view of Saturn's clouds shows storms and strong, swirling winds. The winds blow more than 1,000 miles per hour, much faster than even the strongest winds on Earth.

What lies under the clouds? No spaceship has even been there. But scientists think that beneath the clouds Saturn has no solid surface at all. The weight of the clouds above is very great. It pushes down on the gases in the atmosphere and changes them to liquids. Saturn is probably liquid hydrogen down to its rocky center.

You could not breathe Saturn's atmosphere, nor live in its ocean of liquid hydrogen. Neither could any animal or plant on Earth.

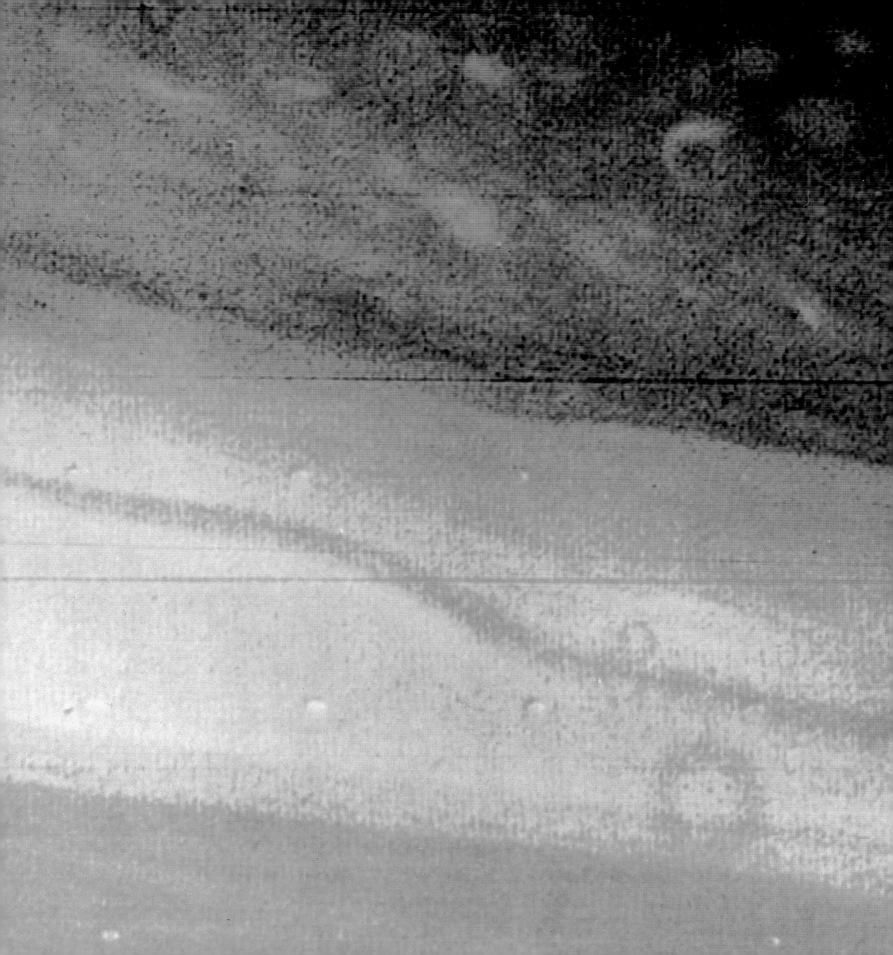

Saturn has more moons than any other planet in the solar system. More than twenty have been discovered, and there may be others. Saturn has one large moon, six that are medium-sized, and many smaller ones. Most of the moons are covered by ice and pockmarked with craters.

This picture of Saturn and some of its moons was made from a number of photographs taken by *Voyager 1.* Saturn is shown partly hidden by Dione, in the front. Enceladus and Rhea are off in the distance to the left. Tethys and Mimas are off to the lower right. And Titan, Saturn's largest moon, is far away at the top right.

Mimas [MY-mas] is the closest to Saturn of the medium-sized moons. It circles the planet once every twenty-two hours. Mimas is about 240 miles across.

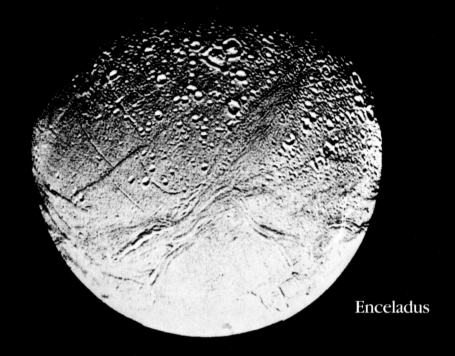

Enceladus

Enceladus [en-SEL-a-dus] is the next outer moon after Mimas. It is about 310 miles across. Enceladus is a puzzling moon. Of all Saturn's medium-sized moons, only Enceladus has no large craters, just small ones. Parts of its surface have no craters at all. Some scientists think that heat from inside the moon melted the icy surface in spots. Water or soft ice then covered the craters and froze over.

Tethys [TEE-this] is about 600 miles across and is mostly ice. It has many large craters, one of which is 250 miles wide and 10 miles deep. This crater is bigger than the state of Ohio.

Another large crater (*lower right*) is the beginning of a giant valley. This continues over Tethys's north pole and down the other side, a distance of 1200 miles.

Some scientists think the valley formed when a huge rock from space crashed into Tethys, splitting open the surface. Other scientists think that the valley formed many years ago when the moon's watery surface froze and then cracked.

Dione [dy-O-nee] is about the same size as Tethys, but it is much heavier. It is made of ice with a rocky center.

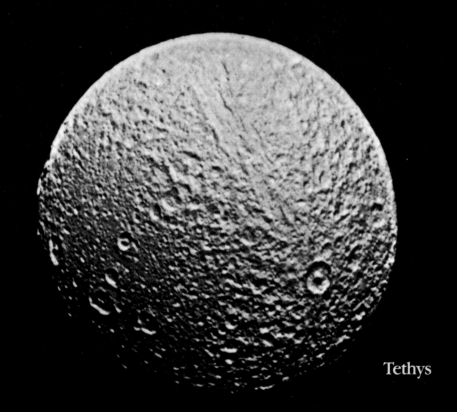

Tethys

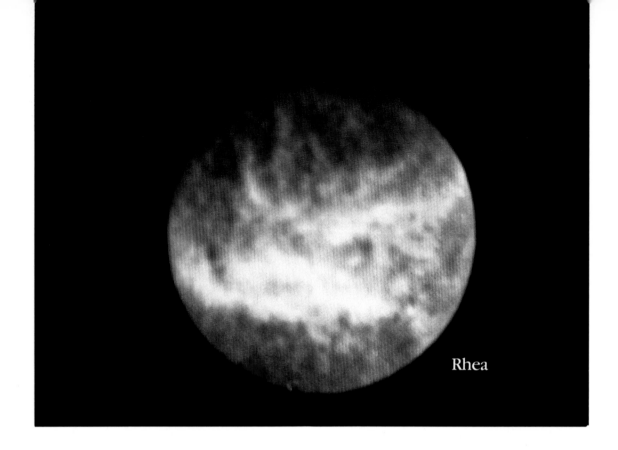

Rhea

Rhea [REE-a] is the second largest of Saturn's moons, about 950 miles across. Like Dione, Rhea is mostly ice and rock. Rhea's surface is heavily covered with craters, the most of any of Saturn's moons. This color picture shows that large parts of Rhea are covered by frost.

Titan [TY-tan] is the largest of Saturn's moons, about 3190 miles across. That's bigger than our own moon and bigger even than the planets Mercury and Pluto.

Titan is the only moon in the Solar System known to have an atmosphere. The atmosphere covers Titan with a thick haze that hides its surface. Titan's atmosphere is mostly nitrogen gas with some methane, a poisonous gas.

Titan is a very, very cold place. Temperatures there go down to 300 degrees (F) below zero. Scientists think that Titan's surface may be covered by thick layers of methane ice and snow. No life as we know it could live on Titan.

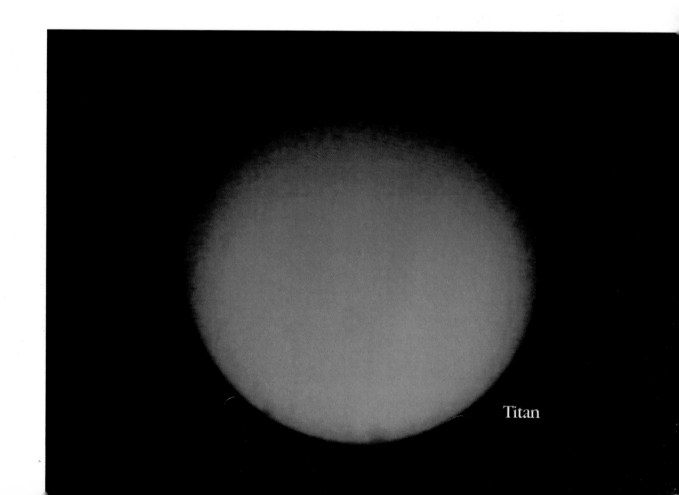

Titan

The three outermost moons of Saturn are Hyperion, Iapetus, and Phoebe. Neither of the *Voyagers* spacecraft took very clear photographs of these moons because they were too far away.

Hyperion [hy-PEER-ee-on] is shaped something like a giant pickle. It is about 250 miles long and about 160 to 140 miles wide. Some scientists think that Hyperion was once a much larger moon, but that another object in space crashed into it and broke Hyperion apart. Hyperion has many craters covering its surface.

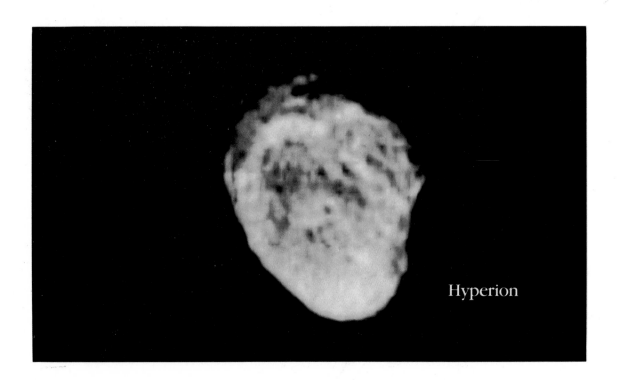

Hyperion

Iapetus

Iapetus [eye-AP-e-tus] is about 900 miles across. It has one side that is much brighter than the other side. The bright side may be ice and the dark side may be rocky. But no one knows for sure.

Tiny Phoebe [FEE-bee] is only about 135 miles across. It is so far away from Saturn—about eight million miles—that it takes 550 days to circle the planet. Phoebe also revolves in the opposite direction from all of the other moons. Perhaps Phoebe was not originally a moon at all. It may have been an asteroid, a rocky object in space, that was captured by Saturn's gravity when it came too close.

This photo of Saturn was taken four days after *Voyager 1* flew past the planet on its way out of the Solar System. Saturn's shadow falls on the rings.

Seen through a telescope from Earth, the ringed planet Saturn is the grandest object in the night sky. And close-up, Saturn's magnificent rings make it the most beautiful of all the planets. The *Pioneer* and *Voyager* spaceships have shown us much about Saturn, its rings, and its moons. But many mysteries still remain to be solved.